Wings above the Sea

A story and images of loss and transformation

Kyoko Katayama

ISBN-13:978-1976099014
ISBN-10:1976099013

For

Eric

Nina, Dimitri, Tamara

1

The waves in the ocean mesmerize me.

I stand on a warm tropical beach,
watching them curl and uncurl.

Where does a wave begin and end?
How do these fluid hills take shape?
What is underneath in the deep blue?

Waves are never still,
endlessly morphing their
speed and foamy crests.

Some merge into others.
Some build momentum
towards their final energetic release,
crashing against the shore.

The sky and the earth
receive each wave

unperturbed.

2

Years ago my beloved and I lay on this beach.

The strong sun and warm breeze kneaded us
into languid, happy dough.

He had just completed a big change in his work.
He made a decisive, uncharacteristic move.

In the seventies he was a dashiki-wearing, clogs clanking,
wild-haired new pediatrician in an inner city clinic.

The white dude with an Afro,
his kid-patients and their families talked of him
with an approving nod.
A black curly mane framed his face.
Twinkling hazel eyes radiated kindness
above his aquiline nose.

Years later, clean-shaven and hair clipped,
he focused on helping
out-of-control children learn self-regulation.
The field was called Behavioral Pediatrics.
His shiny office overlooked a shimmering lake in a suburb.
He empowered a patient's family to be a team with him.
Desperate families gained hope.
Chaos became a rhythm for healing.

Possibilities opened for families.

Eventually the bureaucracy and profit orientation
of healthcare burned him out.
Why not aim to bring lasting health and wellbeing
not just for the kids and their families,
but for the doctor himself?

He left.

In a few months,
he opened a one-doctor office
in a basement near his city home.

Now he could realize his dream.

He was pleased.
He was hopeful.
He was sixty-one.

Warm breeze swayed palm trees,
dappled light in motion.

He reached for my hand.

I looked forward to getting old with him.

Reveries of retiring and traveling,
or spending more time with our grandkids
wafted with the scattered clouds in the blue sky.

Our hands intertwined,
sweat and sandy grit on the fingers.

We cherished being one another's refuge,
sharing deep contentment and dreams.

No reason to imagine anything else.

Near us, another wave crashed and released.

3

A few years before, he had bladder cancer.
The treatment had gone well.
A full remission!

He declared then,
"No more cancer; I had my turn with it.

"Once when I was eight,
my bullying big brother tricked me into inhaling a lit cigarette.
I coughed and spat. I swore I'd never smoke again.

"I eat broccoli and salmon.
I study T'ai-Chi.
I meditate on my black zafu.
There is no reason I should get cancer again."

Back home in the north country,
the lapping of waves still echoing in our hearts,
we got news of his diagnosis.

Stage four pancreatic cancer.

Terminal: A survival rate of one percent.

4

Giant waves approaching.
A tsunami in the heart.

But we were above water,
still breathing.

He ate well and worked with purpose.
He chanced the hope that he could be that one percent.

Those were the early days:
a beginning of our apprenticeship
with Time.

Chemo had not started.

A month after the news,
in the middle of the night
his humble new clinic was ransacked.
Gone were the new computers and office machines.
The hollow spaces on the desks and counters,
yanked cords,
scattered papers
punched his gut,
his sick gut.

They stole the ceramic lizards in the yellow waiting room,
leaving only the exposed nails on the wall.
The sunny memories
of working together to set up the office
blackened.

We stood silent,
we, the eye of hurricane,
the ravaged rooms and body parts spinning
and spinning around us,
gaining momentum.

5

When we began the cancer journey,
Time was an orderly sequence
of past, present, and future.

With each chemo cycle,
with each health crisis,
with each hospital stay,
with each passing day,
the order and certainties of our lives
crumbled.

His visible physical decline
and pain
became our fierce and tender teachers.

Keep on breathing, they whispered.
Do not flinch, they shouted.
Their keen voices between my ears
opened my weary eyes.

They incessantly asked,
What is inevitable?
What is true?
What really matters?

What really matters?

How little we know!
We have no control over when and how our lives end.

Mystery gathered around us,
sometimes looming and swallowing us,
other times rocking us in its misty shelter.

With it came Time,
the shape shifter.

6

Time became a funhouse mirror at the fair.
Our faces scrolled sideways,
our bodies shrank to a pin,
eyes bulged,
mouth puckered to a dot,
all reversed with the slightest move.

Eventually Time became
a thin, illusive line
until it disappeared.

As his cancer progressed,
past and future receded.
Years or months
or even weeks of past and future
blurred.

Out of the dim,
Time gleamed as a bare bone day,
one at a time.

Time was all in our minds.
As Time shrank,
our minds stopped ticking in the ordinary way.

At last, there was just NOW
unfolding
and revealing
what was to be lived
moment
to moment.

7

When Time disappears, what remains?
When the body withers, what happens
to a being?

Not knowing is the ultimate intimacy.

What stands out in my memory of those times
in the midst of sickness
and impending death
was grace.

In the thin place
we found tenderness
and surprising
releases.

8

On the way home from an appointment with his doctor,
we stopped at our favorite Japanese restaurant.
We wanted to do something thick with ordinariness.

None of the chemo was working anymore,
the oncologist had said.
It was time to stop the treatments.
The doctor ordered hospice care at home.

No more chemo!
My beloved felt a strange surrender
and wild freedom,
dancing on the thin ice.

How good the salmon sushi tasted
in the pungent wasabi
and a dab of soy sauce!

His naked head warm in a blue knit cap,
my neck wrapped in a purple pashmina shawl,
to others
we looked like an ordinary middle age couple
planning our spring trip to Grand Canyon.
The illusion pleased us.

They had no idea

that at home a half-hour later
he would vomit two pints of something
that looked like chopped liver
and collapse on the couch.

Our destination was Death Valley.

On the way I learned that vomit, too, is holy.

9

His gaunt cheeks did not
daunt me.
My heart opened
toward his deteriorating body.

Unexpectedly,
astonishingly,
clarity emerged:
I wasn't just taking care of my personal beloved;
I was serving something larger and sacred.
It included everything,
the whole universe,
even
me.

As he was able to do less and less,
in the alchemy of impermanence,
the younger, I-need-you-for-me love
transmuted into shimmering gold.
Something larger
and more trustworthy than our bodies
or our individual selves
held us
in soft,
tremulous
light.

He didn't have to
do anything for me.
His loving glance at me
from the hospice bed
was enough to sustain me.

For eternity, it seemed.

Let go gently, my beloved, of all that holds you back.

As his death neared,
with all my heart
I assured him that,
when the time came,
it was all right for him to go.

I didn't want my attachment to him
to pull him down.
I told myself over
and over,
I will accept
whatever the consequence of this love.

I will accept
whatever
the consequence
of this

love.

11

He exhaled for the last time and slipped away.
His body was taken
from our home,
my entire front half ripped away.

I watched his body slide
onto the grey tiles of the cremation chamber.
His last bed.

Go into the light, my beloved.

Whoosh!
Orange flames lit up and engulfed
the face that kissed me,
the arms that held me.

My beloved turned to ash.

How could he one moment
be alive and loving me,
and in the next
a pile of crushed bones?

The death was brutal, final.

For a year I had walked the razor's edge with him.

Now I was pushed off the cliff.

The world stopped
and everything in it.

I died.

The sky fell and I was a wreckage beneath the crumpled
blue tent.

12

I submitted to being a pile of rubble.

The consequence of love is this, I told myself.

An inner voice whispered,
Don't attempt to get back on the thick ground
where orderly time ticks.
Truth has no time and no ground.

From the bruised bottom,
would I remember
to turn my gaze towards the sky?

In the remote corner of my obsolete brain,
a Zen saying whiffed like a passing cloud.

When the house burns down,
you finally see the clear moon.

13

Everything became a blur.
I was disembodied and lost.
I inhabited the negative space
where he once was,
the space of alternating sharp stabs
and wrecking balls.

How could I bear such pain?

Where did he go?

My mind searched for signs of him,
anything to cling to.

An eagle alighted high on an oak branch.
Is that you?

His favorite mug shattered on the gleaming sink.
Did you do that?

A deer pranced in a green shadow.
Shall I follow you?

They disappeared without an answer
leaving me to scour the vast dark.

When my heart finally grasped his death,
a slit opened and I glimpsed something.

It was like seeing the entire ocean for the first time
in a flash of lightning.
And then darkness fell again.

But the memory imprinted itself,
became an unceasing pull.

In the midst of fragments and losses,
something was untouched by death.

14

High noon in the desert.
Not a cloud in the sky.
The rays of the sun hit my bare arms
like hot needles.
The walk was rough.
I slid on the slope of sharp rocks and spiny cacti.
No sound other than pebbles
slipping under old hiking boots.

When we die what really dies and what lives on?
What does death teach me?
The questions rumbled and clanked
in the rusty bucket of my heart.
They echoed in the hushed desert of Joshua Tree.
Three years had passed since his death.

I trampled on dead creosote twigs,
avoiding the spines of jumping chollas.
Tiny pupils of pink bloomed from the sand.
Their eyes followed my steps, curious.

My exhale, an offering in the arid air.

Inhaling the desert,
an image arose,
perhaps an epigenetic memory,

of pale green tendrils surfacing
through ashes and blackened earth.
A certain sense gathered slowly,
golden filaments connecting the dots
of death, birth, love, time,
timelessness.

Two thousand tons of incendiary bombs dropped in Tokyo.
My mother searched for her mother's body
the morning after the bombing.
In the aftermath of unimaginable devastation,
my mother conceived life,
my life.
I would not have been born if my grandmother had not died
in the sea of fire.
If not for the war that killed a hundred thousand
in one midnight,
I would not have been born.

And then?

15

In the desert, the air quickened.
This was not a renewal of something old,
like the sense of "I" returning.
I as I knew it died with my beloved's death.
I watched his body cease.
My hands held his ashes.
But who witnessed the death of my self?
How do we grieve for a loss
that is a felt sense,
nothing to touch or see?

A tear dropped on a hot rock
and evaporated.
More tears,
for the one who died without a witness.
The whole body heaved,
tearing,
till nothing was left.

Clean and empty, transparent yet moving like wind.

When we die, what lives on? the innocent wind asked.

I took unsteady steps
leaving behind the wet marks drying
on the orange rock.

When I looked up,
a great Joshua Tree loomed above me.
Its sharp green blades poked the blue sky.
Life force spiraled up its solid ridged trunk.
An unquestioning joy
emanated in the luminosity
of the space.

The Joshua Tree recognized me.
In knowing and becoming known,
aliveness soared towards the light
from my own marrow.

What lives on is Life with all its longing.
It is not personal.
Not "I" living but Life living through this body
into a being.

I was born into a new reality:
All the possibilities of being alive!
In radical freedom!

This rebirth would not have been possible
if my beloved didn't die.

A clear and visceral insight arose:
Life and death are one.
Love binds them into seamless unity.

Life, death, and love: Each makes the other possible!

16

Moments before his last exhale
I thanked him for all that he had done.
He helped heal me,
and the family that was broken.

He said, *No, Kyoko.*

His voice was weak but his gaze was clear.

No, Kyoko, we did it together.

As he was readying to leave his body,
as we were bidding farewell,
he reminded me of our unity,
a unity that could not be broken.

Love does not die when we die.

17

The glimpse in the flash
was the glimpse into mystery.

Life, death, and love are one.

Life does not belong to us.
We belong to Life.

Death does not belong to us.
We belong to Death.

Love does not belong to us.
We belong to Love,
eternal, unbound love.

18

I thought I had fallen off a cliff.

When would I crash into a thousand pieces?
I waited to hit the bottom.

Falling and falling, I asked,
When?

Never!
There was no bottom to hit.

A strange opening came with that realization.
I am not falling! I sang out.

This was not a descent towards the lowest earth.
Something was defying gravity.

I was floating
suspended in groundlessness.

At first it was disorienting.
I remembered the time I plunged backwards
into the dark warm sea
at night.

Drifting in the imperceptible current
without any sense of direction,

the eyes saw
and the body merged
with the luminescent and alive
dark waters.

In awe, I discovered buoyancy.

The sea held me in its embrace.

19

In the groundlessness, I wondered
how wings grow.
With wings
I might be able to navigate
this disorientation.

I dreamed
of angels with golden feathers,
of fish surfacing above the waves
and flying across the moon-lit horizon
its wings splashing silver sparkles.

But wings don't grow just because
we want them.

So I remained naked
humility and curiosity my flimsy
cover.

Months passed.

20

One day there was a sensation in my back,
in the space between the shoulder blades.

More time passed.

I felt it again and stronger,
a hand gently and steadily pressing.
Another week, behind me on the left, a sense
of my beloved,
covering my back
with his right hand.

The following day, on the right,
in the regions of scapulae
my mother's left hand.

More emerged as the days passed.
Behind my beloved and my mother,
the invisible yet unassailable light
of my teachers, my benefactors, my ancestors,
buoying me up.

Ahhh…
from there, such a breathtaking view!

21

Beyond the horizon of the sky and the sea
in the prodigious arc of celestial sphere,
scintillating fingers of future children
beckoning,

knowing without reasoning,
sensing without seeing,
a cosmic circle,
an unfathomable
timeless
embrace of

love.

About Kyoko Katayama

Kyoko Katayama was born and grew up in Tokyo, Japan. Although her biological father was an American, she was raised as a Japanese, speaking and knowing only Japanese language and culture. With her mother, she came to the US when she was seventeen.

Since then she has crossed and bridged many cultures. She lived in Italy for six years where some of her children were born. She returned to the US and received her education and training to become a psychotherapist. She has been in private practice since 1994.

In 2010 her beloved husband Eric was diagnosed with terminal cancer. He lived one year from the diagnosis. With the encouragement of a friend, she began painting during this period. Most of the paintings in this book come from that time.

She has been on a spiritual journey since she was a teen. She studied widely on topics related to spirituality, healing, and neuroscience. Since her husband's death, she has become an end of life educator. She is a senior member at Common Ground Meditation Center where she teaches a class, *Befriending Death: Meeting Impermanence with Courage, Love, and Equanimity.*

In addition to teaching Befriending Death classes, she offers her services as a resource and support person for mindful living and conscious dying. She is a member of Minnesota Threshold Network, a non-profit organization dedicated to supporting family-oriented, natural end-of-life transitions.

She has a life-long love and proclivity for visual arts and writing. She began drawing and journaling when she was ten years old and bedridden for a month from an accident. Her poems have appeared in *Asian American Renaissance Journal* and *Intersecting Circles: The Voices of Hapa Women in Poetry and Prose*. An excerpt from her memoir-in-progress was published in *Where the Tree Falls, the Forest Rises: Stories of Death and Renewal* in 2013. http://www.amazon.com/books/dp/1479320374

She is a mother and a grandmother of three delightful grandchildren, and a befriender of a rescue dog — a yellow lab mix who often accompanies her to sessions.

www.skyheartmountain.com

Made in the USA
Columbia, SC
15 July 2019